better together*

*This book is best read together, grownup and kid.

 akidsco.com

a kids
book
about

a kids book about

DIGITAL EQUITY

by Juan Muro, Jr.
in partnership with Free Geek

A Kids Co.
Editor Emma Wolf
Designer Jelani Memory
Creative Director Rick DeLucco
Studio Manager Kenya Feldes
Sales Director Melanie Wilkins
Head of Books Jennifer Goldstein
CEO and Founder Jelani Memory

DK
Delhi Technical Team Bimlesh Tiwary Pushpak Tyagi, Rakesh Kumar
Senior Production Editor Jennifer Murray
Senior Production Controller Louise Minihane
Senior Acquisitions Editor Katy Flint
Acquisitions Project Editor Sara Forster
Managing Art Editor Vicky Short
Managing Director, Licensing Mark Searle

First American edition, 2025
Published in the United States by DK Publishing, 1745 Broadway, 20th Floor,
New York, NY 10019

First published in Great Britain in 2025 by
Dorling Kindersley Limited, 20 Vauxhall Bridge Road, London SW1V 2SA
A Penguin Random House Company

The authorised representative in the EEA is
Dorling Kindersley Verlag GmbH. Arnulfstr. 124, 80636 Munich, Germany

A catalog record for this book is available from the Library of Congress.
A CIP catalogue record for this book is available from the British Library.
ISBN: 978-0-2417-4381-2

DK books are available at special discounts when purchased in bulk for sales
promotions, premiums, fund-raising, or education use. For details, contact:
DK Publishing Special Markets, 1745 Broadway, 20th Floor, New York, NY 10019
SpecialSales@dk.com

Printed and bound in China
www.dk.com
akidsco.com

MIX
Paper | Supporting
responsible forestry
FSC™ C018179

This book was made with Forest
Stewardship Council™ certified
paper – one small step in DK's
commitment to a sustainable future.
**Learn more at www.dk.com/uk/
information/sustainability**

This book is dedicated to the digital equity community and practitioners working tirelessly to bridge the digital divide.

Intro
for grownups

Can you imagine what your life would be like without technology? That would mean no talking on the phone, playing video games, or visiting your favorite website! Having access to technology is GREAT, but sometimes we forget to consider the people around us who DON'T have technology, and how that might impact them.

From doing homework, to talking with friends, to playing your favorite game—technology is a part of everyday life!

If you believe technology is something everyone should have, you're definitely right! My hope is that, by the end of this book, we'll all start thinking more about the importance of everyone having access to the powerful technologies all around us.

Hi, my name is Juan Muro.

I am passionate about technology and love talking about it with my friends, my family, and my community.

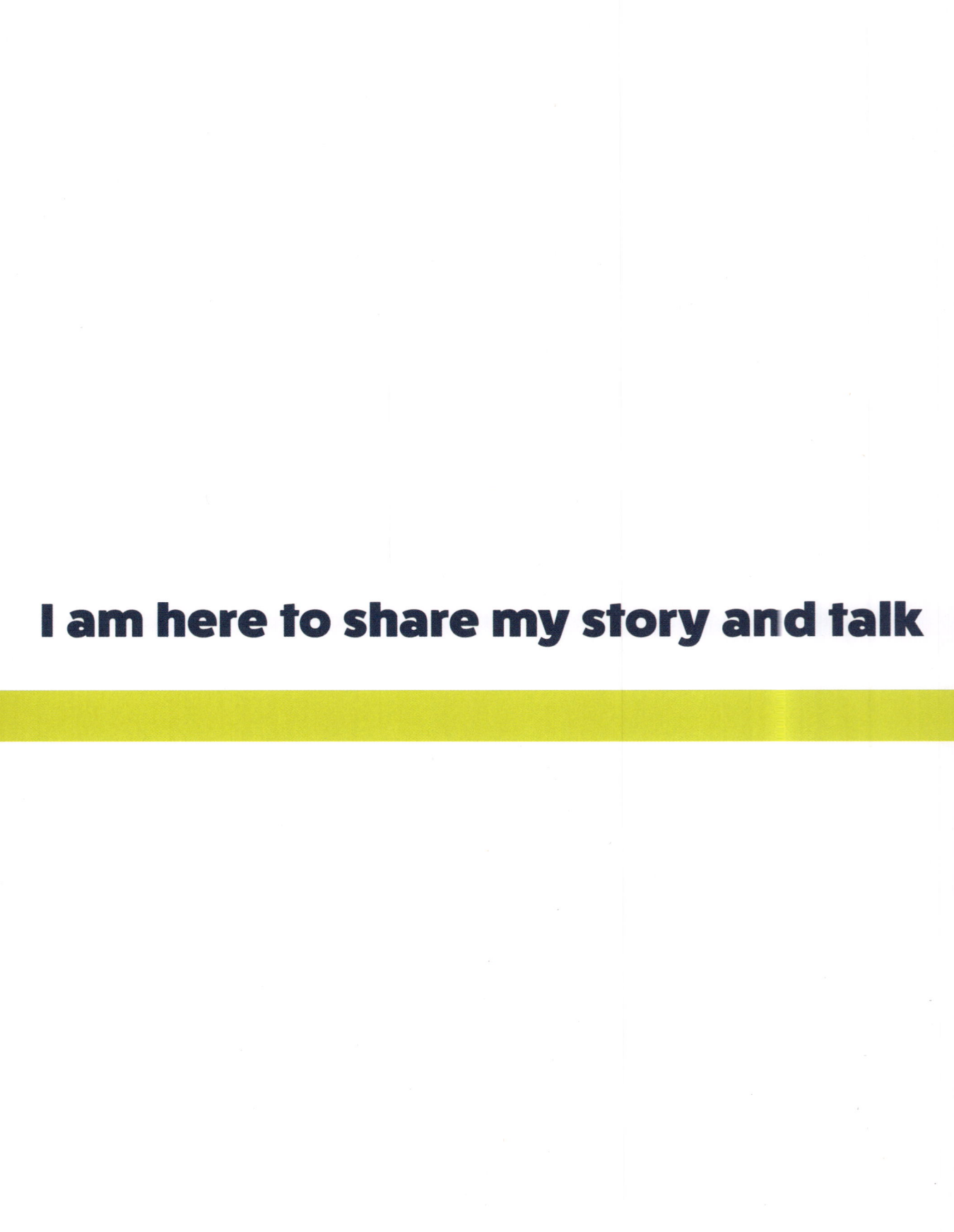

I am here to share my story and talk

about how it connects to digital equity.

I was born and raised in Escondido, California.

Life wasn't always easy.

Sometimes, we didn't have a place to live, or we lived out of my mom's car.

Sometimes, we had a hard time finding the things we needed for everyday life.

But, I still remember my first laptop.

It was a blue, 15-inch Sony Vaio.

And it represented all the possibilities of what my

LIFE COULD BECOME.

With this device in my hands, I felt like I could have a better life.

All because I had access to this little computer.

**Which brings me to
what this book is all about...**

DIGITAL

EQUITY.

My guess is that's a new phrase for you.

You're probably wondering, "What is digital equity?"

Digital equity means everyone has the tools they need to fully be a part of and thrive in society.

Let's unpack that.

What kind of tools
are we talking about?

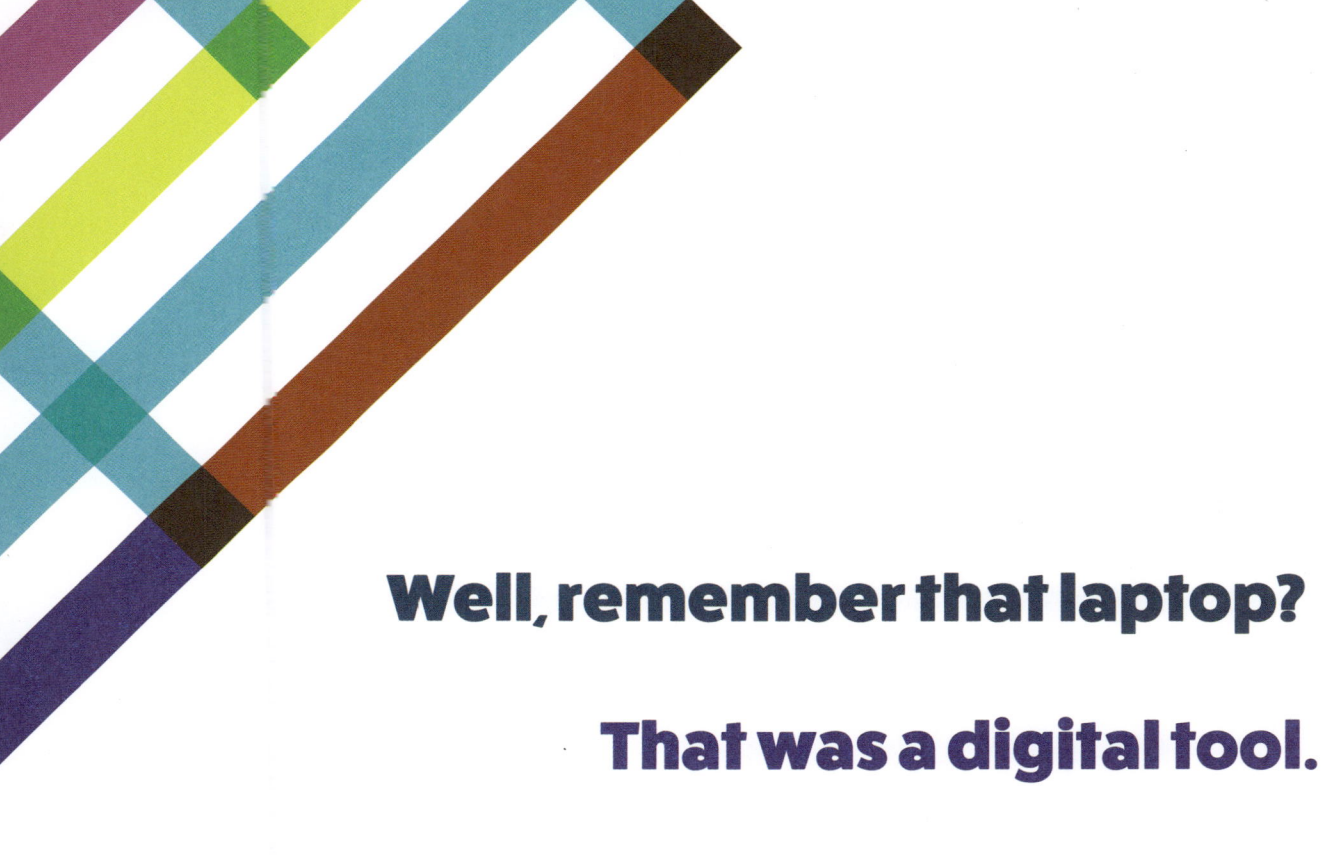

Well, remember that laptop?

That was a digital tool.

Other examples of digital tools are things like cameras, smartphones, desktop computers, and tablets.

These digital tools allow us to create, communicate, and participate in the world around us.

There are so many digital tools like the internet, apps, and software.

They all help both kids and grownups do everything from...

school, to work, to banking, to texting and calling, to travel, to getting all kinds of help.

Maybe this sounds like a totally normal thing everyone experiences.

But I'll let you in on a big secret...

NOT EVER

YONE HAS ACCESS.

This is called the digital divide.

There are way more folks than you think who don't have access to all the digital tools they need.

YES,

including things like smartphones, computers, tablets, and even the internet.

Can you imagine what life would be like without those things?

Go ahead and think about it.

Maybe you're thinking...

No more homework because there's no computer to do it!

That might sound great, but if you don't turn in your homework, you probably won't succeed in your studies.

No more YouTube on the weekends.

(Even if you subscribed to your favorite channel, you can't watch it, ever.)

No more chatting with your friends over summer break.

(You wouldn't be able to text, talk, or video chat.)

No more late-night online gaming.

Yup, sorry.

No streaming music, getting directions, taking pictures, or visiting websites.

Because you don't have the internet or a device that can access it.

Sounds pretty terrible, doesn't it?

Well, over 21 million people in the US don't even have access to the internet.

And even among folks who have internet access, millions of them don't know how to use it.

This creates gaps in digital literacy*, which take us even further away from achieving digital equity.

*Digital literacy is a person's ability to use, communicate, and create with digital tools.

Digital equity doesn't exist for 2 main reasons.

1.

Some of the tools are too expensive.

2.

Some of those tools, like the internet, don't even exist in certain places.

Even though everyone needs these tools, they aren't accessible to everyone.

And honestly, **that's not very fair.**

Worst of all,

the folks this impacts the most are...

People who are Black, brown, or indigenous.

People with low income.

People with a disability.

People who are the most vulnerable, including kids like you.

The hard truth is, when digital equity doesn't exist, and people don't have access to all the tools they need to belong in society...

nobody wins.

So, what can you do about it?!

First, don't ever make anyone feel bad for not having access to digital tools. It is not their fault.

Second, you can always share what you have, like digital access.

If your classmate doesn't have a computer at home, consider inviting them to do homework with you. Always get your grownup's permission first!

Third, speak up to grownups like teachers, parents, and coaches on behalf of other kids so they can have all the tools they need to succeed.

Because we all deserve to fully belong.

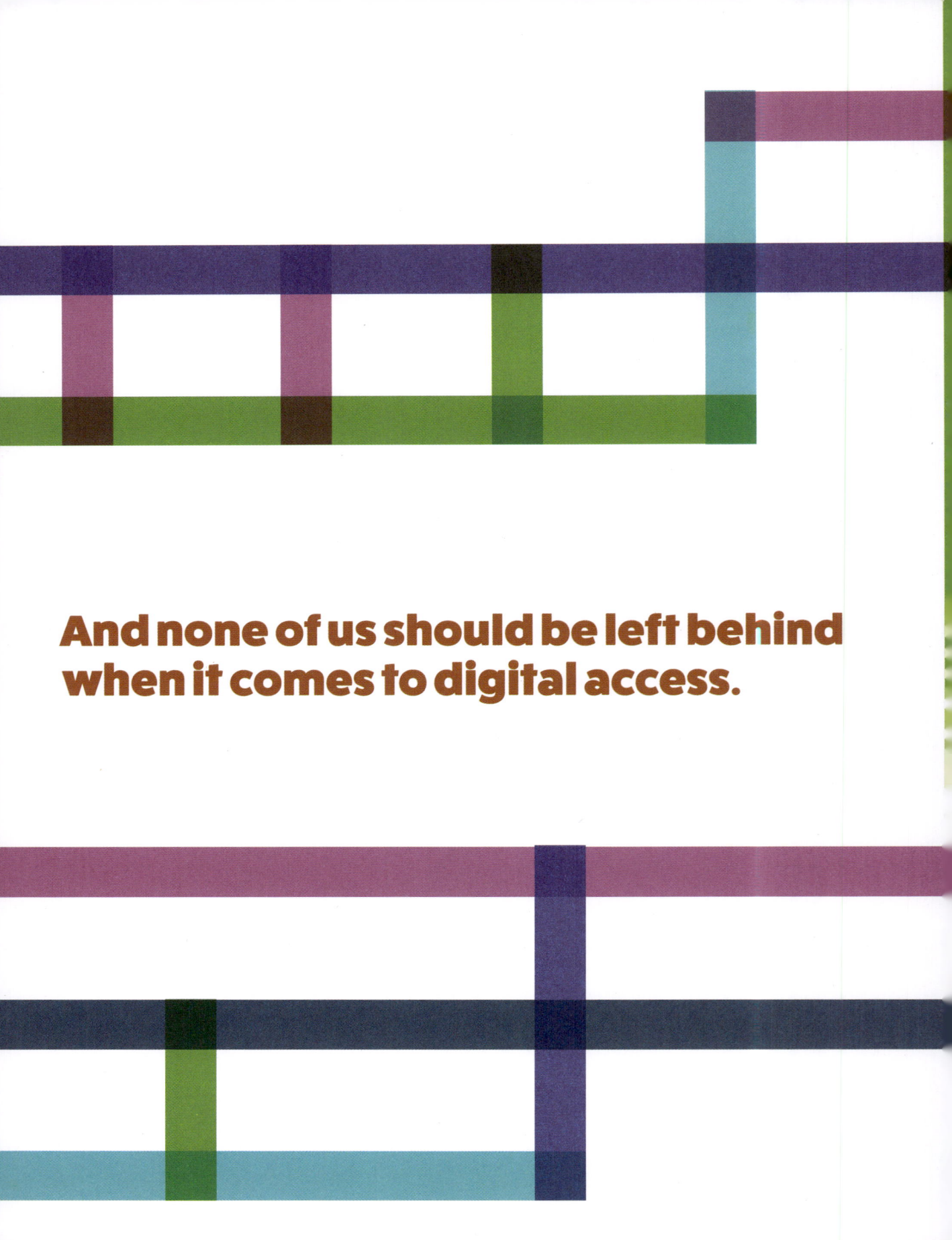

And none of us should be left behind when it comes to digital access.

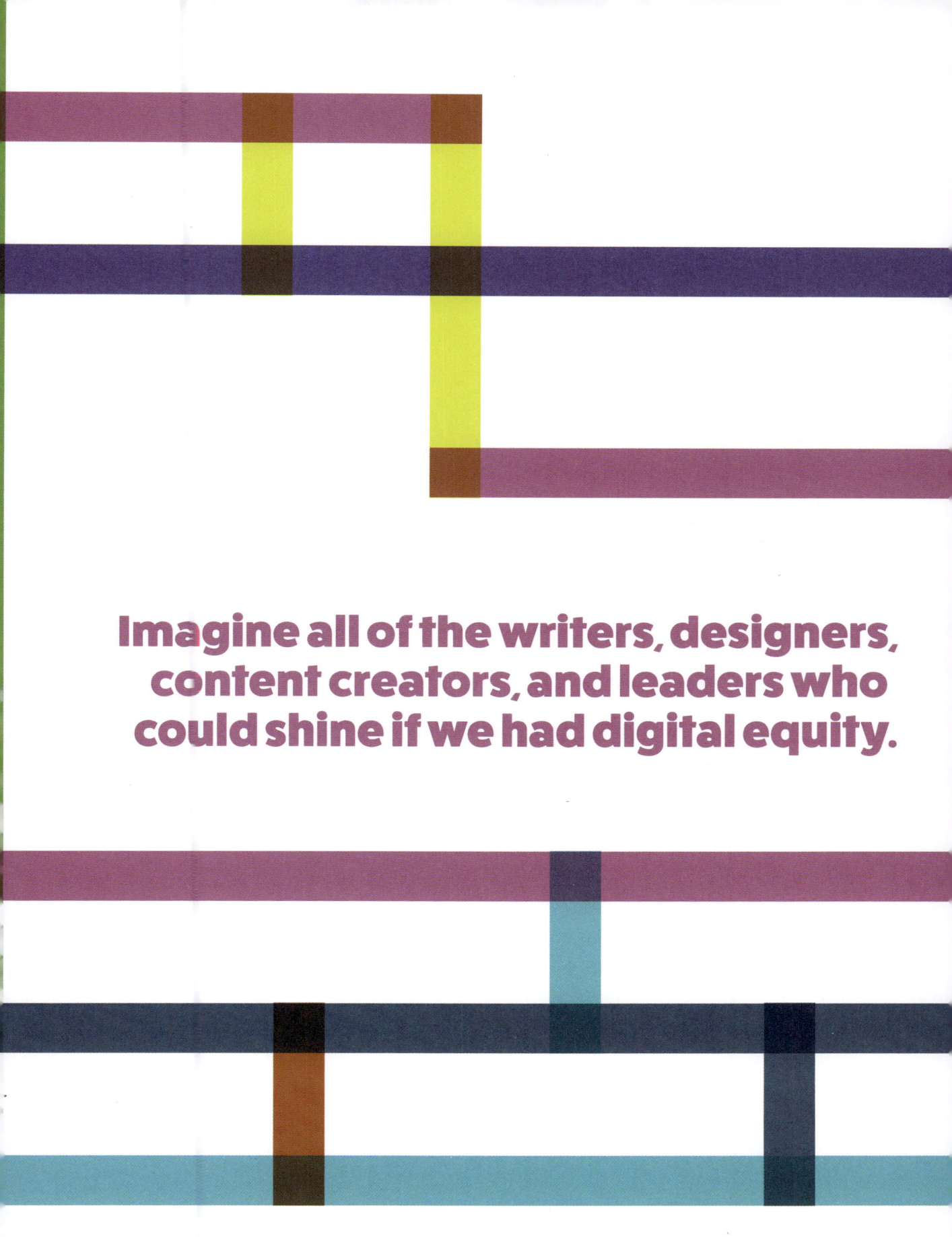

Imagine all of the writers, designers, content creators, and leaders who could shine if we had digital equity.

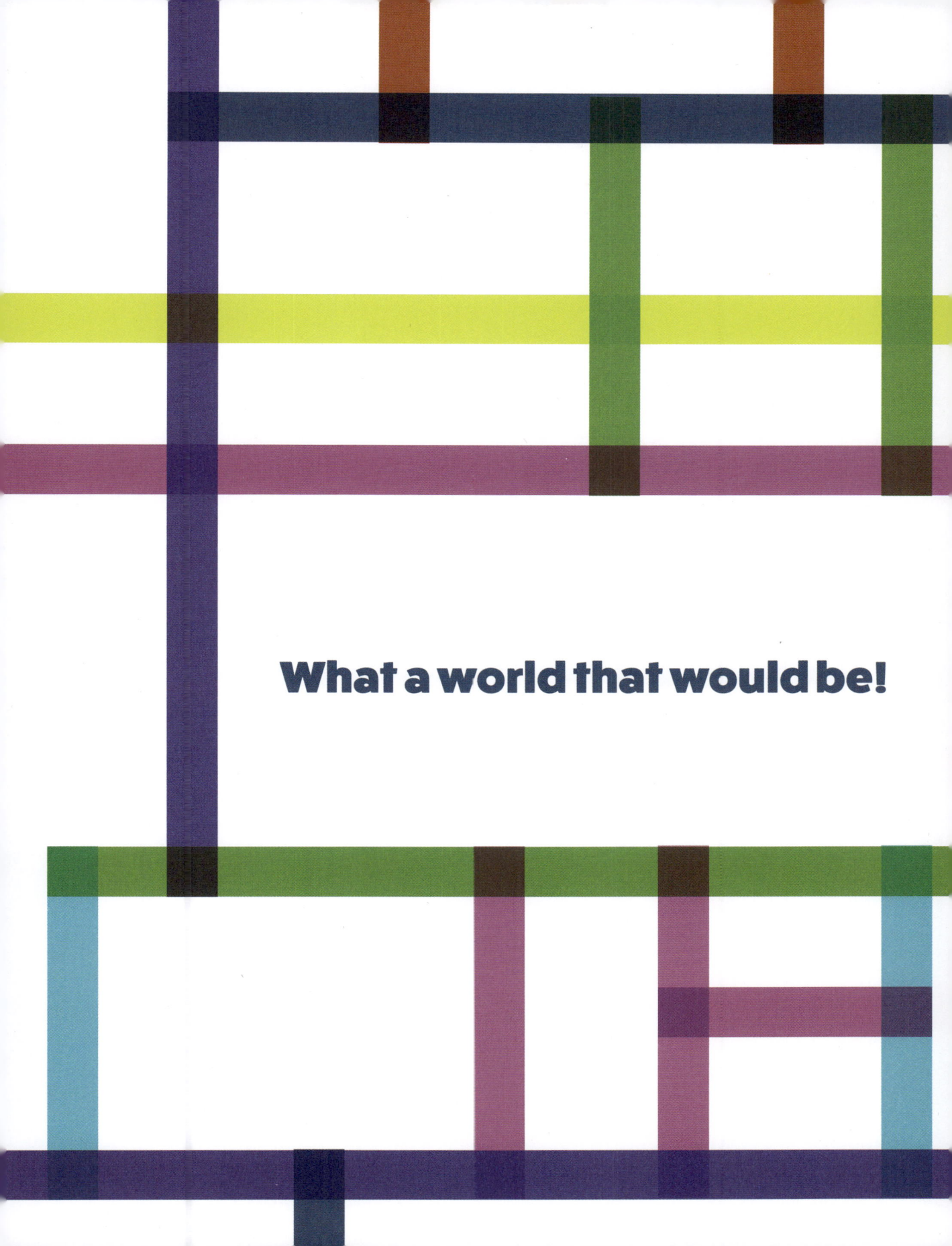

What a world that would be!

Outro
for grownups

Congratulations! You've now learned about the digital divide! What an accomplishment! Now you can use what you learned to help bridge the gap between people who have technology and those who don't.

Technology has become a way of life for most people in the world, yet there are still so many people without access. The good thing is we can all do our part in making sure no one is left behind when it comes to digital access.

Doing something as simple as going to the library with a friend so they can do their homework there can make a HUGE difference in their lives. What else can you do to help improve digital equity in your community?

About The Author

Juan Muro, Jr. (he/him) was born and raised in the underpriviledged neighborhoods of Escondido, California. He moved to Portland, Oregon, in 2017 to pursue work in the nonprofit sector, inspired by his business acumen, leadership style rooted in a "people-first" lens, and ability to build great teams.

Since 2018, he has put those skills to use at Free Geek, a digital equity organization, and has been working to make the programs and community impact better. His lived experience, such as growing up in foster care and inequality, allowed him to witness firsthand the missed opportunities at play when people don't have ample access to technology. With this journey in mind, as the executive director of Free Geek, he is committed to removing technological barriers for those who continue to experience disadvantages caused by the growing digital divide.

 @jmmuro   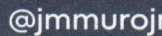 @jmmurojr   freegeek.org

Made to empower.

a kids book about **racism**
by Jelani Memory

a kids book about ANXIETY
by Ross Szabo

a kids book about DISABILITY
by Kristine Napper

a kids book about IMAGINATION
by LEVAR BURTON

a kids book about belonging
by Kevin Carroll

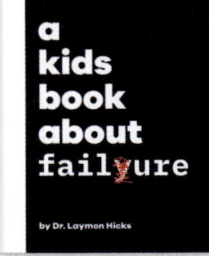
a kids book about failure
by Dr. Laymon Hicks

a kids book about GRATITUDE
by Ben Kenyon

a kids book about LIFE ONLINE
by Dave S. Anderson & Blake Fleischacker

a kids book about body image
by Rebecca Alexander

a kids book about IMMIGRATION
by MJ Calderon

a kids book about EMPATHY
by Daron K. Roberts

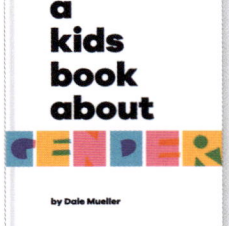
a kids book about GENDER
by Dale Mueller

a kids book about Love
by ZIGGY MARLEY

a kids book about EQUALITY
by BILLIE JEAN KING

a kids book about MONEY
by Adam Stramwasser

a kids book about FEMINISM
by Emma McIlroy

a kids book about adventure
by Dr. Ben Tertin

a kids book about CLIMATE CHANGE
by Zanagee Artis Olivia Greenspan

a kids book about CONFIDENCE
by Joy Cho

a kids book about BEING NONBINARY
by Hunter Chinn-Raicht

Discover more at akidsco.com